Designing and Managing a Training and Development Strategy

PROPERTY OF:

DAVE MELLING

07762 032726

Financial Times Management Briefings are happy to receive proposals from individuals who have expertise in the field of management education.

If you would like to discuss your ideas further, please contact Andrew Mould, Commissioning Editor.

Tel: 0171 447 2210
Fax: 0171 240 5771
e-mail: andrew.mould@pitmanpub.co.uk

FINANCIAL TIMES

Management Briefings

Human Resources

Designing and Managing a Training and Development Strategy

SUE MATHEWS

FT

PITMAN
PUBLISHING

London • Hong Kong • Johannesburg • Melbourne • Singapore • Washington DC

PITMAN PUBLISHING
128 Long Acre, London WC2E 9AN
Tel: +44 (0)171 447 2000
Fax: +44 (0)171 240 5771

A Division of Pearson Professional Limited

First published in Great Britain 1997

© Pearson Professional Limited 1997

The right of S. Mathews to be identified as author
of this work has been asserted by her in accordance
with the Copyright, Designs, and Patents Act 1988.

ISBN 0 273 63199 3

British Library Cataloguing in Publication Data
A CIP catalogue record for this book can be obtained from the British Library.

10 9 8 7 6 5 4 3 2 1

Printed and bound in Great Britain

The Publishers' policy is to use paper manufactured from sustainable forests.

Contents

Foreword

I remember being told by my college tutor midway through my final year that I would work harder in those final months than I would for the rest of my life. Now after a career of 21 years, nothing seems further from the truth!

Many of us face tougher jobs, increased stress, longer hours and continuous demands to produce more, deliver more and deliver quicker; the need to harness strengths, energy and resourcefulness to meet the organization's objectives becomes vital.

We can't keep asking for more from people, but we can help individuals, teams and organizations learn more effective ways of adding value, by giving insights to try new approaches and apply new knowledge and new techniques to enable individuals, at all levels, to question the real value of what they do. It takes confidence to challenge and have influence, to learn to control the roller-coaster and not just sit in the back seat.

Training and development has an absolutely key part to play, but the crucial requirement is that the interventions work. They have to be timely, appropriate and cost-effective to bring about measurable benefits. They must build organizational capability to ensure a focus on constant improvement, improvement that is noticeable to the customers and employees and is reflected in growth, increased profits and more effective cash management.

Getting training and development right can add substantially to an organization; getting it wrong can be a costly waste of resources.

This training and development management report covers a thorough, systematic approach to delivering real benefits from training and development. It asks the questions, it makes you think, but above all, it gives practical insights into how we can build better organizations. It's a real 'tool box' approach – what could be more useful to busy managers? I warmly recommend this report to you.

David Phelps
Human Resources Manager
Danisco Pack Ltd

About the author

Sue Mathews has a BA (Hons) degree in History from the London School of Economics. She is a Member of the Institute of Personnel Management and the Institute of Training and Development and is on the Board of the European Women's Management Development Network.

Sue has spent most of her professional life in Personnel and Management Training, with extensive experience in the UK, Europe, Africa and the Far East. Her previous employers include: Uniroyal Ltd, National Mutual Life Association and the Hong Kong and Shanghai Banking Corporation.

She is Managing Director of Training By Design, a Human Resource Management Consultancy, which has an international client list whose activities include: broadcasting, local government, various aspects of industry and commerce and creative and design bodies. She is also a founding Director of Media Associates, a media communications company.

In particular, Training By Design has developed a worldwide reputation for its work on organisational development through diversity, with particular focus on the enhanced creativity of organisations which have design as a core function.

She has written articles for a number of publications on subjects ranging from management skills for women to 10th century Anglo-Saxon art.

The author can be contacted at: Training by Design, Telephone: (01993) 891 720, Fax: (01993) 891 589.

1   An introduction

Staff Development – Why Bother?

'If you think training is expensive, try ignorance.' This is a favourite quote of mine when dealing with individuals or organizations whose first reaction to a downturn in trading or profit is to slash the staff development budget.

Staff development is how any organization, large or small, public sector or private, equips itself with people who have the necessary range of knowledge and skills to achieve the current purposes of their jobs and to create a reservoir of abilities for their career goals.

Staff Development as a Core Corporate Strategy

Like any other essential organizational requirement for the maintenance and promotion of profitable growth, development and training in all its forms should be a part of the core organizational strategy, closely tied into the business plan, assessed, reviewed and revised like all the other corporate strategies. Effective development is not an accidental, haphazard, *ad hoc* process, but needs to be a carefully thought out, highly synchronized series of activities carried out throughout the organization by various appropriate methods.

The more an organization genuinely values its people and their varied contributions towards that organization's success, achievements and well-being, the more that organization is prepared to invest in its staff's learning. That conviction is reflected in the demonstrable commitment by all managers, particularly, and especially, at the very top. Senior managers can send out the message that 'we are serious about the value we place in our people and their learning' by committing funds, through properly managed and accountable training budgets, by encouraging their staff to have development experiences and by giving their time by being mentors and coaches to more junior staff.

Training Policy

Any organization which is genuinely and seriously committed to offering its staff a range of developmental experiences, not only for the organization's benefit but for the benefit of the staff members themselves, should have that commitment made public in a Training Policy. The Training Policy, like any other corporate policy, such as Equal Opportunities, Health and Safety, Career Advancement, etc., needs to be clearly supported by senior managers and included in the Annual Report and any other appropriate formal corporate publication.

The Cost of Ignorance and No Training

The national media and the training press are constantly full of stories which reflect the sad fact that as a nation we all receive less training than our European counterparts, particularly the lower down in the hierarchy we are. Senior managers receive roughly double the amount of development experiences and two-thirds the formal training of a shopfloor supervisor in the same organization.

A report published at the end of 1995 identified that only half of the UK's top blue-chip organizations actually provided any IT training for their staff. It is a cliché of the 1990s that the IT revolution is one of the biggest and most important factors in most organizations' strategy, yet here we are being told that we invest in the technology, but we don't support that investment with a further and complementary investment in training the people who use it: net result – less efficient and effective use of the technology = big waste of money!

Who to Involve?

Whilst it is highly desirable that there is a focus of overall control and accountability for the processes to achieve the development objectives, training does not always have to be carried out by specialists. Training is now at the stage where finance was about 15 years ago. Until then the only people in organizations who could read a balance sheet, make sense of the profit and loss account and plan a budget were the finance specialists.

Now, any manager worth his/her salt will have been on at least one 'Finance for Non-Financial Managers Course', will feel at ease in talking figures and will almost certainly have control over her/his departmental budget, including its preparation and presentation. In other words, finance is no longer seen as

the exclusive preserve of the finance department, but has in at least some of its areas been devolved down to the managers, with executive control for the management of the processes, the standards and the strategy remaining the territory of the experts.

It would help all development if it became a much more integrated part of organization, if more line managers and supervisors could be actively involved not just at the analysis stage (through assessments etc.) but also in implementation.

What's the Difference Between Training and Development?

All training is development, but not all development is training! All planned learning experiences, formal and informal, could be called development. Development could include a period of secondment, posting to a special assignment or project, receiving a piece of delegated work, being coached or mentored, informal workplace learning as well as attending formal 'classroom' training courses.

Training is specifically the formal element in the entire development process, either in the workplace or in another locality. In this report I will be using both words more or less as I have described them above.

The Objectives of this Report

I want this report to be a practical 'tool box' approach to all the issues related to the identification of training and development matters for individuals and their organizations, showing how to correlate these requirements into a cost-effective, outcome-driven, measurable Training Plan, and then how to implement that plan. It is aimed not just at training specialists but any line manager or supervisor who has responsibility for the development of her/his staff.

2 Building up the development profile of an organization

The raw material for an effective exploration of the development needs of an organization lies not in the personnel and development department or in the personal files of the staff, but within the overall strategy and corporate goals of that organization. The essence of a really effective development plan balances the needs of the organization with the needs of the individual staff members. Before considering the individual requirements of the staff group, the organization needs to be completely and unequivocally clear about issues of business and organizational direction. Unless the organization is clear about these vital topics, whatever methodology is used to establish the individual development needs, the eventual development plan will lack cohesion and direction; it will potentially fail because it is not matching the balance of the two sets of requirements. The development plan must be placed in the context of the 'big picture'.

What Sources?

- Business plan

- Marketing strategy

- Health and safety policy

- Equal opportunities policy

These formal documents will provide the framework of information and direction around which all development activities should be clustered.

Additionally, other sources which should feed into the development plan could include:

- technological innovations and other new equipment purchases;

- research and development issues for new products;

- new market development;

- any expected overseas expansion;

- an analysis of what the competitors are doing;

- an analysis of what may be missing from the skills repertoire at all levels;

- induction requirements for intakes of new staff;

- staff in staffing levels (redundancies can create a skills crisis for the remaining staff).

All this information should contribute to the overall picture of where the company is going, new product development, the market place, its profit aspiration, the staffing implications and the organizational structure.

When preparing the criteria for assessing how successful the development activities have been, the skills requirements indicated through the above will create the most accurate and most relevant checklist for measuring effectiveness, reducing much of the 'guesstimate' approach to development activities appraisal.*

---

* See also the report entitled *The Assessment and Evaluation of Training* by I. Pearce (Technical Communications (Publishing) Ltd, 1995).

3 Analysing the development needs

There is always a terrible temptation to begin in the middle or towards the end of the development process by *starting* with a training course. The all too frequent path by which training is offered to staff is that someone senior has decided there is some sort of crisis. The answer to the problem is usually seen as training, so the training manager or an external trainer is then brought in to solve the problem. Often there are short-term gains in the acquisition of new information, some regenerated enthusiasm and even a genuine commitment to 'do things differently' in the workplace. However, as we all know, the beneficial effects of the training soon wears off, sometimes reinforcing the stereotype that 'training really doesn't work'.

Of course, under such circumstances no training is likely to be successful; that is, it is unlikely to achieve the objectives for which it had been intended. The simple reason is that, like any other strategy activity in any organization, all staff development activities need to be part of a continuous ongoing system. The system need not – indeed should not – be slow or ponderous, generating paper and problems; nevertheless, the investment in staff development will show a much higher return if there is a recognizable and manageable system.

Knowledge and Skills vs Personal Development

Knowledge and skills are directly related to the tasks and functions listed in the job description, and will include technical information, marketing, accounting, IT and other computing skills, recruitment and selection, continuing professional development, supervisory, equal opportunities, health and safety, management and leadership training. Personal development covers such topics as communication skills, assertiveness, time management and stress management. In other words, there are skills which can also enhance the life of the individual outside work and can be considered therefore as 'life or social' skills.

Workplace Standards

A prerequisite for the effective implementation of any staff development plan is the existence of well-publicised, universally understood, achievable and accepted workplace standards. All development activities need to be placed within the context of these standards. It simply is not helpful to say to

someone 'Do this faster/better' unless 'faster/better' can be qualified in a way that is measurable. The workplace standards referred to here are made up of a combination of degree of accuracy and speed/frequency/number and conform to pre-established criteria.

Objectives and Outcomes

The first stage is simply to be clear about what objectives you are seeking to accomplish in engaging in this activity. Is it to develop career plans for high fliers? Is it to identify skills gaps (i.e. the 'what's missing')? Is it in response to a crisis? Being clear about why you are engaging in this will help you 'quality control' the process and outcomes as you progress.

Who is Responsible?

In an organization large enough to have a personnel/development department, the natural choice would be the development/training manager to plan, co-ordinate and project manage the process. However, the research activities should be carried out wherever possible by the direct line managers for all one-on-one interviews, and by trained staff for any group activities.

An important part of the process is to make sure that staff know why the training needs analysis is being carried out, what their role is and the likely outcomes of their involvement. Team briefing sessions and notices in the staff journal and on the office e-mail will all help to let staff know what is happening and will increase their willingness to participate actively.

The next stage is to gather sufficient information for a clear profile of the organization's development needs, in priority order and demonstrably linked to the requirements of the business plan. This is the stage often ignored by organizations because it can be time consuming. However, it is well worth the investment in time and effort; it help makes sure that the future investments in time and money deliver what the organization and its people need.

There are three key ways of building up an effective profile of the development needs of an organization. These are discussed in the following sections.

Ongoing Supervision

This is the process by which managers and supervisors actively keep in touch with their staff on a formal, managed basis.

Supervision should not be an intrusive activity with the manager hanging over the shoulder of a staff member, but should take the form of a series of planned private meetings between staff member and direct line manager (or supervisor), with the permanent objective of creating an open discussion forum about the staff member's current performance issues.

These supervisory sessions are not only concerned with workload management and direction of the tasks, but also should include discussions about issues which are of concern to either person and the remedial action necessary.

Such remedial action could, for example, be either closer work review by the supervisors, additional coaching from another staff member, some formal training, further recommended reading, etc., whatever it takes in fact to improve the performance and bring it up to the required standard. The development information gathered at these sessions can then be fed into the larger organizational development process. These sessions should be recorded ideally by both, but at least by the manager, and kept in a secure and confidential place.

Appraisal Schemes*

These days, most large organizations have some sort of staff appraisal scheme, sometimes linked to salaries/bonuses, sometimes not. However, more and more smaller companies are seeing the worth of using a process which allows a formal annual discussion between staff member and manager in which the staff member's performance is reviewed in order to assess the future development requirements, not only of that individual, but also for the organization as a whole. An appraisal interview is definitely not the place nor the time to raise issues of such a serious or urgent nature – they should have been dealt with elsewhere and earlier. In effect there should be no surprises at an appraisal meeting.

---

*   See the report *Performance Appraisal* by B. Wynne (Technical Communications (Publishing) Ltd, 1995).

CASE STUDY 3.1 An appraisal scheme

Documentation recently developed for a medium-sized firm of architects in East Anglia, Ruddle Wilkinson Ltd, is reproduced by kind permission in the Appendix at the end of this report. This appraisal documentation formed part of a staff development process which was initiated in 1995 as a part of their Investors in People application and other continuous staff development systems. Ruddle Wilkinson's other staff development initiatives are described further in Case study 3.2 below.

The Ruddle Wilkinson Ltd Appraisal Scheme has a number of interesting features:

- it is neither linked to a salary nor a bonus scheme;

- it focuses much on the individual's performance within the team;

- it uses a scoring mechanism to summarise performance in order to avoid subjective use of language;

- staff members complete a copy of the appraisal form beforehand, so creating a discussion rather than a manager-driven monologue;

- it is clearly linked to the job description so everyone can see what criteria and topics are being covered;

- it clearly indicates the desired levels of improvement in both performance and behaviour, using the same scoring system;

- its focus is on achieving a balance between the company's development requirements and the individual's career aspirations;

- it creates data for the annual training needs analysis;

- its overall direction is forward.

Training Needs Analysis

Training needs analysis (TNA) is a misnomer because it indicates that only formal classroom training is covered by its remit. In fact an effective TNA should cover all aspects of development. A TNA is the structured process carried out by a variety of different methods by which information about an organization's development and training needs is gathered, then reviewed and codified as the basis for the development plan.

If the organization already has an appraisal scheme in place, much of the raw data can be compiled from that. However, there might well be other development issues which have not emerged during the appraisal process or which are not on an individual's development agenda.

In each approach the objective is to gather development data relevant to the needs of the business and of the individuals within it, from all sections of the target workforce for a known and agreed period of time, i.e. the next 12 months, the next calendar year or the next financial year.

Who To Ask?

You may not wish, because of the time and administration effort, to ask everyone about their development requirements, so you may need to pre-select some staff.

How To Do It?

- **Diagonal slice.** You can randomly target two or three people at each level of the organization, thus covering every grade but not necessarily every function. The random selection element is important as it stops bias creeping in.

- **Vertical slice.** You can randomly select two or three people in every grade and in every function, thus you cover every grade and every function, but might have quite a few people to talk to.

- **Benchmark functions.** In benchmarking functions for TNAs you will form random sample groups of people in similar functions, i.e. all computer staff, all financial/accounting staff, all clerical/secretarial staff, not necessarily representing all levels of grade within that function.

- **By workplace unit.** In this you will simply use the organization's own hierarchy of corporate, division, department, group or team and have sample staff from each unit.

Which Method?

- **Training surveys or questionnaires.** These can be used to canvas the whole staff group or any one of the groupings indicated above.

- **Individual interviews.** These can be very useful but require time and staff sufficiently well skilled in interviewing to elicit information.

- **Group workshops.** Using the groupings indicated above, the staff are invited to identify their development requirements in interactive workshop sessions. This is much more rewarding and involving for the staff, offering them a greater opportunity to commit to future development opportunities.

Whatever method you select, bear in mind that staff often view TNA's with some anxiety, as these are frequently seen as a criticism of their current performance.

Topics To Be Covered

- Specific function or behaviour to be addressed, including all 'component parts'. If this is a new function or behaviour requirement (such as dealing with equal opportunity issues), some thought will need to be given to informing the staff about the detail of the new function and where/how it fits into their current workload.

- Standard to be achieved.

- Problem areas which may be found, i.e. dealing with difficult customers.

- What skills/abilities are required to reach desired standard.

- What training has been received to date and people's view/recollections of this training.

- Views about the staff's opinions on the most useful training development format.

- Priority in relation to other development requirements.

- Any other contributions from the staff.

Possible Pitfalls

- **Communication.** Staff are not told what is happening and why, so they speculate, gossip and get it wrong.

- **Objectives.** The objectives and expected outcomes have not been thought through properly, so the process becomes unfocused and loses direction.

- **Project management.** No one is taking clear responsibility for driving the process forward; it's being carried out by committee perhaps, and there is no effective accountability.

- **Method.** The method chosen was not appropriate for the objectives and desired outcomes.

- **Expectations.** TNAs raise expectations that something useful will happen as a result; if nothing occurs, staff will almost inevitably see the process as a demonstration of poor leadership by senior managers.

CASE STUDY 3.2 Training needs analysis

The following is an extract from the full report on the training needs analysis for director and executive development at Ruddle Wilkinson Ltd, the East Anglian firm of architects. It is reproduced with kind permission.

The Brief

The brief to Training by Design was to develop, design and present a series of development exploration modules for the existing Directorate and Associates/Architects at RW. The modules have both short- and long-term objectives for both groups. The assignment forms part of RW's

---

long-term, five-year plan under the Investors in People scheme to promote one or more of their own staff to senior levels.

The perspective on which this assignment has been based was that of 'corporate achievement', that is a group of individuals, functioning as a team, clearly working together with shared values, the same goals and mutual understanding of strengths and weaknesses.

Development Objectives

Directorate

- Develop clear understanding of 'top team's' strengths and weaknesses

- Develop profile of skills 'gaps'

- Create an agenda of skills required to manage the 'gaps'

- Develop profile of company/top team values and vision

- Create an RW entrepreneurial checklist as a benchmark against which to assess both the existing 'top team's' entrepreneurial achievements and for potential 'high fliers'

- Create a profile of the 'profit' issues

- Create individual development agendas for each member of the top team

Associates/Architects

- Assess their career anchors (i.e. career aspirations)

- Compare/contrast their performance against the entrepreneurial checklist

- Assess their skills in relation to the skills audit with the 'top team'

- Prepare an individual training needs analysis for each delegate

- Where appropriate, make recommendations for future development/career advancement/promotion

Expected Outcomes

- Reinforced 'top team' corporate commitment

- Coherent, clear agenda of skills development issues for the 'top team'

- Communicable vision of RW values

- Profit- and people-focused entrepreneurial checklist

- Promotion plan for some staff

- A careers development plan for named staff

- A less stressed, more organized group of managers

Methodology

The methodology used was a combination of individual and/or group activities, largely centred towards the answering of prepared questionnaires. The questionnaires themselves were designed not only to reveal information, but also to generate discussion. The individual sessions followed the same process; individual questionnaires followed by a discussion with the consultant.

Summary of Activities

Directorate

- RW:
  – SWOT analysis (strengths, weaknesses, opportunities, threats)

- Directorate:
  - Swot analysis
  - Skills audit (management, leadship, professional and commercial)
  - Company values profile (i.e. what's important to RW)
  - Team type analysis
  - Directorate development profile
  - Profit issues

Associates/Architects

- Personal values activity

- Careers audit

- Skills audit

- Measurement against entrepreneurial checklist

- Individual training needs analysis

4   From analysis into a plan

What To Include in a Development Plan

A development plan should be kept as simple as possible, and be factually based rather than a fancy wish-list of activities which may or may not take place. The development plan could include:

- timespan covered by the plan;

- sources and methodology which informed the plan;

- the overall development objectives;

- the responsible personnel;

- the development and training topics plus their objectives, contents, outcomes, duration and location;

- how to select the appropriate development session;

- who should attend training programmes;

- the development outcomes expected;

- standards to which the development is aimed;

- development assessment criteria;

- timetabling, i.e. dates;

- budgetary information;

- how to have access to a development activity.

CASE STUDY 4.1 Ruddle Wilkinson Ltd Director and Executive Development Programme 1995–97

Below is the list of contents for the above, indicating what was covered and summarising the development analysis activities (described elsewhere in this report) leading to this development plan for the directors and senior managers. In the ordinary course of events the budget costs and other information would be included in the development plan.

List of Contents

1. Introduction: the brief to Training By Design
    - Methodology

2. Corporate development issues
    - Communication/corporateness
    - Team development
    - Delegation
    - Profit/growth
    - Standards

3. Directorate development issues – general
    - Values and vision
    - RW SWOT
    - Directorate team – SWOT/team styles
    - Skills
    - Profit issues
    - Entrepreneurial benchmark profile
    - Conclusions and recommendations

4. Directorate development issues – individual
    - Each director's training and development requirements

5. Associates'/architects' development issues – general
    - Corporate values
    - RW SWOT
    - Conclusions and recommendations

6.   Associates'/Architects' development issues – individual
          – Each associate's/architect's career aspirations, training
            and development requirements
          – Conclusions and recommendations

7.   Summary: consolidated recommended training and
          development programme for next 24 months

CASE STUDY 4.2 Ruddle Wilkinson Ltd Director and Executive Development Programme 1995–97

Below is section 7 of the report: 'Summary: consolidated recommended training and development programme for next 24 months'.

Training module	Directors	Associates	Architects
Personal skills			
Communication	X		
– Relationships	X	X	X
– Negotiations	X	X	X
– Presentations		X	X
Time	X		
– Prioritizing	X		
– Meetings	X		
– Delegation	X	X	X
– Problem-solving	X	X	X
– Planning	X	X	X
Stress management	X	X	X
Assertiveness	X	X	X
Leadership team development			
Leadership/people management	X	X	X
– Controlling }			
– Directing }			
– Motivating }			

Training module	Directors	Associates	Architects
Staff appraisals	X		
Managing change	X		
Building teams	X		
Standards	X		
Managing conflict	X		
Project management		X	X
Coaching/Training	X		
Commercial			
Marketing	X	X	X
Finance	X	X	X
Client partnerships	X	X	X
Team development	X		
Company communication	X	X	X
Client relationships	X	X	X
Profit 'Profile'	X		
Project management	X	X	X
Standards	X	X	X
Quality	X	X	X

Development Headings for Inclusion in the Plan

Depending on what the needs analysis has revealed, the development plan could include development headings such as, for example, the following:

Training courses	Duration (days)	Location	Dates	
Technical/professional skills				
Word processing	2	Head Office	1–2	Mar
Computer programming	5	Head Office	lst/2nd week	Apr
	(over 2 weeks)			
Sales skills	2 residential	London	4–5	May
Equal opportunities	2 residential	London	8–9	June
			8–9	Oct
Health and safety	1	Head Office	16	Apr
			11	July
			25	Sept
Business French (beginners) } Business French) (advanced)	see Training Department for details			
Managerial/leadership				
Basic management skills	3	Cardiff	tbc	
Finance for non-financial Managers	5	London	1–5	July
			24–25	Nov
Leadership skills	4	Cardiff	9–12	Sept

Building teams	3	Head Office	3–6	Oct
Managing discipline	5	Head Office	20–25	Oct
Outward bound programme	3½ residential	Wales	1–4	Dec
Communication skills				
Interpersonal communication	2	Head Office	17–18	Mar
			8–9	Oct
Negotiation and influencing	2	London	6–7	Apr
			14–15	Nov
Presentation skills	2	Cardiff	22–23	May
			18–19	Jan
Report and letter writing	1	Head Office	23 Nov	
Dealing with conflict	1	Head Office	30 Nov	
Working on the telephone	1	Cardiff	10 Dec	
Personal skills				
Time management	1	Head Office	on the 13th of every month except Jan, Aug, Dec	
Stress	1	Head Office	1	Apr
			1	July
			1	Nov
Assertiveness	2	London	5	Apr
			5	July
			5	Oct

External Courses

If you know of any external courses which are directly relevant to your, and the company's development plan, please contact the Training Department with the course information.

New Staff Induction Programme

A three day programme which commences on the first Tuesday of every month in the Head Office, Cardiff and London. Please contact the Training Department for the Induction Programme pack.

Development Activities

- Coaching and mentoring by various board directors

- Special project management assignments

- Three months' secondment to the Paris Office

- Three months' secondment to the Cardiff sales team

- Three months' secondment to the Managing Director's Office

- Three months' secondment to the Training Department (to pilot a Training the Trainers Pack)

- One year's part-time secondment to the local College of Further Education to develop their computer training packages

- One year's special assignment to the new Staff Induction Training Team in all three induction centres

- Four places are available for company-sponsored MBAs – please see the Training Department for details

Evaluation Measurement Criteria

It is useful to include information in the development plan about how the development activities on offer will be evaluated and the role of the staff member in that evaluation. Those criteria could include:

- degree of increased conformity to standard required, i.e. number of customer complaints reduced to nil in a three-month period;

- level of achievement against workshop objectives and expected outcomes;

- intangible results such as increase in personal confidence;

- increased profit performance, i.e. increased sales;

- increased product production, i.e. exceeding quota.

All development activities should have clearly stated objectives and some measurable outcomes generally; then, for each attendee there should be, as a result of dialogue with the line manager, some agreed personal objectives against which the development activity can be measured.

Timing/Timetabling/Synchronizing

Training and development activities can be like Number 22 buses: nothing for years and then everything comes at once! It's pointless to offer specialized training for the accounts department just as the year-end comes into view, or to plan a team building programme for the marketing department in September, usually the busiest time for most marketing departments. Similarly, from the time the schools break up in July until they go back in September it is almost impossible to get enough people together to make an open programme a financial possibility.

So the first rule in timing and timetabling is not to schedule activities at known times of commitment, business or in the holiday period. The holiday periods include the two weeks before Christmas and two weeks into the New Year, at least a week either side of Easter and through the summer holidays – and bear in mind the important religious festivals for some faiths.

The second rule in planning the development timetable is that staff will not want to be absent from their workstations all the time to be on development

sessions. Try to stagger the variety of different formal sessions over the period covered by the plan so that all residential programmes are not crammed into the autumn.

The development opportunities should also be synchronized to offer maximum learning by providing the skills before they are required, i.e. training on a new software package would be more useful before the package is expected to go on-line.

Linking Development Opportunities with Development Requirements

An essential element of staff accessing the development activities is how the connection and correlation is made between what has previously been identified through one-on-one supervision and/or staff appraisals and what is now currently on offer. This initiative should come from the staff member's line manager.

The line manager should take responsibility for setting up a discussion with the staff member using the appraisal/supervision notes and development plans as the agenda. Together with the staff member, forthcoming development activities should be planned in order of priority.

Development Costs

In preparing the development plan, the cost factor will be a significant issue. The costs might include:

- fees for external trainers for certain activities;

- travel and accommodation costs for external trainers;

- equipment hire (if not already owned);

- capital investment in purchase of equipment;

- hire of venue (if no on-site facilities are available);

- purchase of ready-made development materials, i.e. CD-ROM, computer packages, trainers' kits;

- overnight/residential accommodation for residential courses;

- fees for attending public 'open' programmes;

- stationery costs for materials, folders, visuals etc.;

- some organizations also include the cost of staff salaries for either attending activities or for in-house coaching/mentoring;

- the cost of the Training Department and its staff.

All these costs will build up into the overall budget.

Development Budgets

In a perfect world the development activities on offer would be controlled by the needs of the people of the organization, but of course in reality it is money which is really the arbiter.

When compiling the development plan a decision will need to be made about the control of development budgets.

- Is there to be one development budget for the whole company controlled by the Training Department?

- Are there to be separate budgets for different separate development topics?

- Are there to be separate budgets for each department controlled by that department?

- Are there to be corporate budgets for certain activities, i.e. 'open' programmes and departmental budgets for departmental activities?

Keeping Staff Informed

The development plan will be the corporate strategy which dictates all development activities; however, like any other corporate strategic document you will need to consider if all parts of it need to be published company-wide. A decision needs to be made about which bits of it should be published and which not.

This decision needs to be viewed in the light of how far honesty, candour and openness is a part of the corporate culture.

By and large the contents of the development plan should be available to everyone, so that staff can be clear about what the organization is seeking to achieve. After all, if a company is prepared to invest time and money in a needs analysis in order to genuinely offer some effective, useful learning to its staff, their cooperation both at the analysis stage and at implementation is essential. And the best way to encourage wholehearted involvement is by open frankness and honesty.

Traditionally it is the senior manager in a department who has the copy of the organizational development plan and it is through him/her that staff hear about the development activities on offer. However, this can be potentially a very limited method of providing access to the information, as the manager can control who has that access. Some of the other methods of publishing the development plan which can be used singly or collectively are:

- prepare it as a brochure with a copy for all staff;

- hold communication cascade meetings to brief staff on the development plan;

- post as e-mail to all staff;

- post to e-mail noticeboard;

- send memo to all staff telling them who holds the plan and how to access it.

Senior Management Involvement

Like any other significant corporate activity, the more senior managers are seen to be actively involved (but not interfering) in the activities and process, the stronger the message of 'we are serious about this'. Further, the more senior management are engaged with the process, the more they are likely to 'stay on board', that is maintaining their commitment and encourage their staff to exploit the development opportunities on offer.

The sort of activities in which senior managers can engage are:

- hosting briefing sessions about the development plan;

- becoming mentors and coaches;

- attending training and development sessions as delegates;

- becoming tutors on some programmes;

- 'topping' and 'tailing' training courses;

- giving and receiving feedback about development activities;

- ensuring that everyone in their departments is able to attend whatever development opportunities have been previously discussed with them;

- engaging in the discussions about standards and workplace quality issues;

- making sure that there is a viable and sufficient training budget.

5   From a plan into action

Plans are all very well, but they are just a waste of paper if their contents are not translated in viable reality. In this chapter I would like to explore a number of issues related to turning your development plan into useful learning experiences for your staff.

From Paper to People

In the previous chapters I spoke about the importance of keeping everyone informed about all stages of the development plan, involving them wherever possible in contributing to the formulation of the contents. Now, at the 'point of delivery', the urgency in maintaining dialogue with your staff continues.

The all too familiar process by which people end up on a training programme is that their line manager decides there is a problem, either sends the staff member on an external course or selects a training course from the company's development plan. The staff member is then expected to come back to the workplace fully motivated to implement all the new ideas he or she has learned on the training course: net result = frustrated and suspicious staff member + disappointed line manager.

A more useful process could be:

1.   Using either the staff appraisal and/or the regular supervisory sessions, staff member and line manager together identify an area requiring development.

2.   Jointly they agree what the workplace standards and issues are, the development objectives and the specific expected outcomes.

3.   They agree on the format of development which will best suit the requirements of (2) above.

4.   One or both takes responsibility for finding out what's available either in-house or externally, together with costs etc.

5.   Together they review all the development information available in order to make an informed and shared decision.

6.   When they agree the particular development experience appropriate for achieving their objectives, they should agree specific targets and the feedback process. (NB: key decisions should be noted, either in the individual's Training Record or in the supervision notes, whichever is the usual. Some organizations record all this as a Training Contract, i.e. the staff member agrees to achieve certain objectives through the development experience and the manager agrees to create an environment where the learning can be put into action.)

7.   Staff member attends the development activity.

8.   Debriefing takes place with the line manager to assess achievement against objectives, plan implementation and identify any further supervision or support requirements.

This process may look a lot longer, but in fact it's probably no more than three or four conversations over a period of time. It's an effective investment of both the manager's and the staff member's time and other resources.

In other words the actual development activity is like the bit of the iceberg you can actually see – it's held vertical and in place by the huge mass, unseen but stabilizing beneath the water's surface. Without this investment in time and enthusiasm by the line manager, the development activity will simply not be anchored in the working practices for that staff member – it will not achieve its goals.

Impact on the Workplace

I sometimes wonder why the £1.5 billion spent annually in this country on workplace staff development doesn't have more effect. Of course one of the major reasons is that the development activities in the plan are either not structured to translate the activities from paper descriptions via the learning experience to permanent and meaningful changes in the workplace, or that the workplace itself remains hostile to any deviations in behaviour by the staff member, no matter how much lip-service is given to the importance of flexibility and responding positively to change. It's a waste of money and time investing in any development at all if the workplace environment remains rigidly unyielding or unsympathetic to the effort of personal change that the staff member might be trying to make as a result of the development sessions.

Training expert and learning guru Peter Honey in his column in the April 1996 Edition of *Training Officer* (partly reproduced below with thanks to Peter Honey and the *Training Officer* magazine) describes clearly why even the best formulated of development activities can sometimes fail to maintain the learning momentum back in the workplace.

Learning situation	At work
The top priority is to learn; it is a carefully contrived learning environment.	The top priority is to produce and achieve, with learning as an accidental spin-off.
The objectives are explicit and there is an obvious link between means and ends.	Objectives are often vague and much of what happens is unconnected or contradictory.
Trainers have no real clout, their leadership depends on securing consent via interpersonal skills.	There are managers who ultimately control 'bread and rations' and have the power to demand compliance or else.
It is relatively safe to have a go, experiment and make mistakes.	It is only safe if people are cautious and minimize the likelihood of mistakes.
It is deliberately structured to capture people's interest, stimulate participation and value their efforts.	It is deliberately structured to maintain control over the processes that produce goods and services.
Win–win behaviours are actively encouraged and reinforced, such as mutual support, openness to ideas and helpful feedback.	Win–lose behaviours are condoned such as 'put downs', 'not invented here' attitudes and back stabbing.
Interruptions and distractions are minimized.	Interruptions are the norm.
Seniors are absent (or only allowed access at set times for a specific purpose).	Seniors are everywhere breathing down people's necks and constantly meddling.

Maintaining the Enthusiasm

This section could have been called 'Creating a Learning Organization'; this is because, without doubt, for the enthusiasm for learning to be maintained, it is not enough to have a great training plan, committed, skilled and dedicated tutors/trainers, a willing staff, clear objectives or even a huge budget – it is absolutely essential that the organization itself, that is all the people in the organization, be committed to learning.

Energy, willingness and vigour will soon dissipate if the efforts of individuals are not received into an organization, large or small, where learning is seen as a connected, ongoing, purposeful process, a dignified achievement in its own right.

Peter Honey goes on to say further in the July/August edition of *Training Officer* that 'creating a learning organization is simple, but not easy' and that the essential step is to make learning a genuine priority at work instead of it being an accidental by-product.

Once learning is a priority, the processes of learning become self-conscious and connected to other forms of learning rather than being a series of isolated incidents. Peter Honey suggests a useful checklist to help this process (published below with thanks to Peter Honey and *Training Officer* magazine):

- Analyse mistakes to see what can be learned from them.

- Ask people what they have learned today and what they are going to do differently tomorrow.

- Delegate – not just to get the job done but to give someone a development opportunity.

- Get someone to do your in-tray for you and review with them the decisions they made.

- Get people to experiment with new and different ways of doing things.

- Require all project group/task forces to report 'lessons learned' in addition to their recommendations.

- Use meetings as opportunities to learn from the processes, not just from the agenda items.

- Get people to set monthly learning/development objectives and agree how you can help them achieve them.

Avoiding Development Overload

Recently, on a training programme for senior managers, I was very concerned that one particular manager seemed worryingly lethargic and appeared to be unresponsive to the activities, so I shared my concern with her during one of the breaks. Her reply was that she was sure the programme was fine – in fact she had been looking forward to it – but as this was the second course this month, with another scheduled for the next month (all with pre-course work), two special projects waiting for her back in the workplace and a trainee about to be seconded to her department, she had other development matters on her mind. Development overload indeed!

In your enthusiasm to share all the glittering prizes of the development plan, please make sure that the delegates have enough time to put their new learning into practice. You should also bear in mind that, although theoretically they should have delegated much of their workload and other in-flow is being diverted elsewhere, the reality for most staff is that the work simply continues to pile up whilst they are away learning new skills.

Don't overload them – development needs to be a steady, planned process allowing time for delegates to reflect, inwardly digest and then practise. Further, the longer the gap between the learning and implementation, the more likely it is that the delegate will either forget or lose motivation to try the new skills out.

Reviewing Overall Objectives and Performance Measurement Criteria

Quoting Peter Honey again (*Training Officer*, June 1996), using the model of 'Plan – Do – Review – Conclude – Plan' will stand you in good stead when reviewing objectives and your performance measurement criteria. The key is to move away from reviewing everything at the end of the experience; try rather to instigate the review process as part of the learning itself:

Plan	=	Development plan and individual training contracts.
Do	=	Explicit learning model, learning activities and exercises, training logs and in-training learning reviews.

Review	=	Dialogue to examine, measure and assess outcomes in relation to objectives, using the logs and in-training learning reviews.
Conclude	=	Summarize the conclusions reached by the delegate and his/her line manager.
Plan	=	Agree how the learning is to be implemented in the workplace.

Training Resources

It's always useful to double check all the training resources before the development plan gets under way. So, as an *aide-mémoire*, the definitive training resources list (including the essentials as well as some fancy wish-list items) is as follows:

Venue

- **Accommodation.** Rather than waste your precious time hunting around for hotels and venues suitable for your development activities, use a venue finding service. It's free to clients, and saves much time.

- **Room layout.** The room layout will depend largely on the number of delegates attending, style of programme and content. The usual seating is U-shaped with the trainer's equipment at one end. The debate continues whether or not delegates should have tables; personally, as people usually have desks to work at, and I see all development activities as a variation of work, I prefer delegates to have desks. Generally the larger the room the more comfortable people will feel, especially if natural light is available.

  You will need 'break out' rooms for small group activities, unless the plenary room is large enough. It can actively reduce the effectiveness of a programme if the room is too cramped and the delegates too tightly packed in – it is a false economy.

Facilities

Your venue/accommodation will need to be able to provide an appropriate mid-day meal, bearing in mind that many people are non-meat eaters. Fresh water should be in the training rooms, plus tea/coffee at stipulated times. Easy access for staff with disabilities is essential. Parking is another important requirement.

Equipment

You will need to have available:

- flip charts and endless supplies of paper (you may wish to consider wall-mounted white boards);

- a million multipurpose felt-tip pens;

- video for CCTV replays and commercial videos;

- TV monitor (for use with above);

- screen for use with overhead projector;

- carousel projector with spare carousels (plus remote control);

- microphone and stand (plus lapel mikes);

- overhead projector (or two, one of which could be portable);

- computer facilities to support presentations;

- lectern/podium OHP-making facility;

- plenty of spare acetates;

- wall-mount available for flipchart notes (instead of 'Blu Tack');

- place name cards;

- name badges;

- training packs for notes;

- 'Post-It' stickers;

- message board with pins;

- black-out curtains for rooms with overhead projectors etc.;

- writing paper;

- blank training logs;

- pens for delegates;

- audio loop for hearing-impaired delegates;

- materials in braille for sight-impaired delegates;

- training resource library;

- study rooms.

6 Troubleshooting – making sure everything works

There are a number of reasons why development plans fail to get off the ground:

- development is seen as low priority, a political topic rather than a strategic issue and therefore not valued in the organization;

- there are no development/training standards;

- there is no continuing evaluation of all development activities;

- there is inadequate control of development budget(s);

- there is no effective briefing by managers of staff attending development sessions;

- staff are not released to attend programmes;

- the development activities on offer are not adequately marketed internally, so no one hears about them;

- marketing material fails to adequately describe the development opportunities in such a way that potential delegates/attendees see the value and relate the possible learning to their own circumstances;

- the development activities fail to meet any identified development need, so no one signs up for them;

- the content of the programmes fails to match the 'marketing' hype;

- sessions are cancelled, either because staff don't show up or pull out (or are pulled out) at the last minute;

- trainers/tutors/facilitators are not skilled enough, fail to have the appropriate information or are poorly briefed;

- no effective administration to ensure smooth management of the development processes.

An Accountable Person

Many of the problems described briefly above could be eradicated or at least resolved in the early stages if there is someone in the organization – someone senior – who is seen to be directly accountable for the development function. Traditionally, this is usually the Director of Human Resources/Personnel, but if there is not such a person, this could just as easily be handled by, say, the Director of Marketing or Operations or indeed the Managing Director him/herself; it just depends on how much the organization values its people and their development.

The seniority of the accountable person is important because for development to be given a priority in the organization, it must get onto the 'top team's' agenda, and for that to happen, development needs a powerful sponsor. This sponsor needs to be able to argue the development case for time, money, resources, commitment and energy from his/her colleagues, not just when the organization is profitable and on a 'high', but also when the going is rough and the shareholders are getting restive.

Further, the accountable person needs to be able to 'chivvy' (in the nicest possible way) his/her colleagues into making sure that their commitment is genuine and that staff will be released for whatever development sessions they require.

As such, the accountable person is accountable for:

•   keeping development permanently on the board's (or equivalents) agenda;

•   maintaining the organization's commitment to development;

•   correlating the business goals with the development objectives;

•   coaxing funds for budgets out of the Finance Department;

•   instigating development policies;

•   instigating systems, processes and people to implement development plan(s);

•   formulating development plans with his/her development team;

•   instigating the criteria for the selection of external trainers/ tutors/facilitators (and maybe their recruitment too);

•   instigating the standards for all development activities;

- communicating development objectives, policies, processes and plans to the board and to the staff;

- setting the style, tone and pace of all development priorities within the organization;

- leading the development team;

- being accountable for the success or failure of the development plan.

A Responsible Person

Many of the other problems described previously are connected with not having someone in the organization responsible for managing the processes and the systems. This responsible person, often to be found in the HR/Personnel/Development Department (but could as easily be located elsewhere, perhaps with other complementary administrative duties), has a key role to play in enacting the policies, procedures and processes instigated by the accountable person. Policies, procedures and processes need vigorous and active implementation by someone who can 'get things done'.

As such, the responsible person is responsible for:

- managing/enacting the policies, procedures and development processes;

- managing/enacting the communication process of all aspects of the development plan, including:

  - marketing activities;

  - booking places on programmes;

  - maintaining dialogue with attendees;

  - sending out briefing materials to managers and staff;

  - managing the evaluation process;

  - collecting/disseminating information on relevant external development opportunities;

- maintaining the record system of all staff development experiences;

- managing/procuring the administrative development infrastructure: venues, accommodation, equipment, stationery, facilities, etc.;

- monitoring development budget(s);

- managing development financial requirements;

- managing internal requirements/external trainer interface;

- synthesizing all development evaluations for summary to the accountable person.

Policies, Procedures and Processes

One way or another you will need to have some sort of method of managing the development activities, so you will need some systems.

Development Policies

These should be candid, clear and easy to understand statements about what staff development means in your organization, what the development activities are seeking to achieve and how this is to be done, the rights and responsibilities of staff, and the various people to speak to about getting further information.

Development Procedures

These, usefully, could be published together with the development policies and should cover the practical nuts and bolts of all aspects of the development plan, as well as how to access development activities, specific development objectives, evaluation and monitoring processes, appraisal schemes, training needs analysis, development and training standards, how to access external and specialist courses, and what to do if staff feel they are not getting fair and equitable development treatment – everything, in fact, which staff will need to know about all aspects of development within the organization.

Development Processes

The essential objectives for creating processes for managing the development function (other than those already covered) are as follows:

- how to let people know what development activities are available, i.e. the current development brochure;

- how people book to get onto an activity;

- how development standards are created;

- how activities are evaluated and monitored;

- what is done with the information collected through evaluation and monitoring;

- the evaluation and selection of external trainers, etc.;

- how to effectively manage the development budgets.

Development Standards

In previous chapters I spoke of the importance of establishing workplace standards so that all the development activities have a directed focus and a means to measure achievement. There is, however, another set of standards which will contribute much towards the successful accomplishment of the development plan – and these are development standards.

A major contributor to the lacklustre performance of development activities and the resulting negative feedback is the lack of standards for such activities. This allows poor practice, shoddy training performances, unhelpful support materials and irrelevant sessions to occur.

The sorts of standards which you might like to consider for your development activities could include the following:

Administration

- All enquiries replied to within seven days.

- All staff given eight weeks notification of a forthcoming development activity.

- All nominations for places responded to within seven days.

- All delegates to receive programme information at least 14 working days before the commencement of the activity.

- All staff development activities to be recorded.

- All complaints about any aspect of the development process to be responded to within seven days.

Development Resources

- All external training information updated every three months.

- All trainers'/tutors'/facilitators' files updated every 12 months.

- At least three tenders from external resources for all development activities.

- Standard selection process, including formal presentation, for all development tenders.

- Every 12 months all external trainers/tutors/facilitators have to be re-evaluated.

Development Processes

- All staff have a pre-development activity session with line manager.

- All staff have a post-development session with line manager.

- Line managers have to provide reasons, in writing, to the accountable person for withdrawing a delegate from a programme with less than five working days' notice.

- Standard, detailed development evaluation forms are to be supported by verbal 'diagonal slice' post-activity assessment debriefings.

- All tutors/trainers/facilitators must write a detailed report of the development activities together with an analysis of the evaluation forms.

- All development activities and their trainers/tutors/facilitators are given a full on-site evaluation by an attending member of the development team every 12 months.

- All tutors/trainers/facilitators must recieve an average of 'good' (or equivalent) or above on the activity assessments for every programme they run; if they fall below, their role on that programme would need to be carefully reconsidered.

- All development materials must be checked by the Staff Development Department before use.

- All development support materials must be printed and prepared to an agreed format.

- All support materials must be on corporate stationery.

7 The 'hit list' of ten essential actions

If you don't have the time/money/energy to do anything else, please try to find the resources to 'do' these ten essential development actions:

1. **Keeping everyone informed**
    Sound development is not just concerned with providing activities, but means setting a good example, and one of the best examples anyone can provide is that of sound and effective communication. Development, like anything else generated by 'management' in organizations, is always the subject of much gossip and speculation, sometimes accurate, generally not. So, take the initiative and keep everyone informed using a method which really delivers the information quickly and accurately.

2. **Clarity of overall and specific objectives**
    When you are effectively communicating with your staff about your development plans, some of the most useful topics you can discuss with them are the overall and specific objectives of the development plan – its strategy and tactics and what this means to them and how these objectives were formulated. This will help people understand what you are doing and why, and relates the development plans to their own requirements. Of course, this does mean that you need to have thought out those objectives first.

3. **Understanding by everyone of expected outcomes**
    The next most important point you need to communicate to your staff is that each development activity carries with it expected outcomes, i.e. what is expected to be different as a result of the development experience, and that staff will be measured in relation to how far those outcomes have been met.

4. **Realizing that all problems cannot be resolved by training or development**
    Fundamental to effective development is the honest understanding that many organizational problems cannot be resolved by training because they are not development issues but problems generated by other things, such as poor or inadequate resources, inappropriate systems or structures, or shoddy products. Lack of knowledge may contribute to these problems, but development/training could only ever deal with the short-term symptoms of these sorts of organizational defficiencies.

5. **Clear and measurable development performance criteria**
    In other words, make sure that all your development activities perform to agreed standards and criteria before they are implemented with your staff, otherwise the investment in development will never be returned.

6. **Recognizing that training is a core corporate issue**
    Bring development in off the margins of importance and priority in your organization. Make sure that someone important is accountable for it; include development in the 'top team's' agenda and gives it a decent budget.

7. **Development should not iust be for the 'stars' of any organization**
    Development opportunities must be genuinely and realistically available for all members of staff, not just for the favoured few being 'groomed' for stardom. The development plan must ensure that all members of the workforce have fair and equitable access to development which is relevant for them. If not, the development plan is not working.

8. **Don't make development an additional organizational stressor!**
    In any busy organization, large or small, the last thing anyone wants is one more activity, no matter how worthy, to add to their workload. If you want people to get the most out of the development opportunities, make sure that you support them in managing their workload so that when they return they are not swamped: otherwise, development becomes an organizational stressor and no one will want to take the risk of attending the activities because of the hassle awaiting them upon their return – a major development demotivator.

9. **Be prepared to sell your development ideas**
    Not everyone in your organization will share your missionary zeal for development – to lots of people it is just another cost off the bottom line. So, be prepared to actively 'sell' the benefits of your development plan. It is essential that you honestly convince senior managers of the absolutely essential role development has in the organization and that their support is central to its success. So hone those selling skills.

10. **Correlate the development activities with the bottom line**
    This is closely linked to 9 above. It will help you to 'sell' your development plan if you are clearly able to demonstrate how closely the plan springs from and supports the profit (and other corporate) issues. Be prepared to argue strongly the business case for the development plan – after all, it's the reason why you have it.

Appendix: Documentation for Ruddle Wilkinson Ltd staff appraisal scheme

RUDDLE WILKINSON LTD
STAFF APPRAISAL SCHEME
PERFORMANCE AND DEVELOPMENT

Section 1

Name .... Job Title ....

Period covered by this Appraisal ....

Length of time in current job ....

This form completed by ....

Staff Member's Signature .... Director's Signature ....

Date of Appraisal Discussion ....

Section 2

Job Description Objectives:	Team Building Dispositions:
1.	1. A resolve always to value one's own skills and those of others.
2.	2. A willingness to listen and to communicate honestly and purposefully with one another.
3.	3. A commitment to help and encourage one another.
4.	4. A readiness to extend trust to one another's team leader, who earns this trust by striving to maximise the team welfare and performance.
5.	5. A feeling of responsibility for the team as a whole as it works for the successful completion of a worthwhile task.
6.	6. A willingness to contribute one's own creative inputs and to allow them to be transformed into other, better team outputs.

Job Descriptions Key Functions:	Team Key Functions:
1.	
2.	
3.	
4.	
5.	
6.	

Job Description Significant Relationships:	
1.	
2.	
3.	
4.	
5.	
6.	

INSTRUCTIONS FOR COMPLETION OF APPRAISAL FORM:

ADMINISTRATION

To support the staff in completion of this form the whole of this section is also included on the Appraisal Form itself.

Frequency: appraisals will be held twice yearly: February/March
September/October.

Confidentiality: the appraisals are strictly confidential and, once completed, will only be kept in the official Personnel file, held in 'John Smith"s' office. No one other than 'John Smith' will have access to the completed Appraisal Forms. The only copies of the Appraisal Forms to be taken will be the back page 'Development Action', copies of which will be held by the appraiser and the appraisee only

Staff Involvement: the staff member will be given a blank appraisal form to complete before the interview, so that the ensuing discussion has a focus. Staff members must retain their own copies.

Appeals: staff have the right to a further discussion with the Board if they significantly fail to agree the majority of their Director's appraisal of them. The Board will then nominate two other Directors for appraisal appeals.

Documentation: the appraisals completed by the Directors must be hand written; Directors must not retain copies for their own staff files. Staff will be asked to sign the appraisal form to indicate agreement with the contents, if they refuse they can appeal (see above).

Development Agenda: The last page of the form, page 5 section 5, heading Development Action must be detached from the rest of the form and kept by the appraising Director with a copy held by the staff member to provide the agenda for the forthcoming supervisory sessions.

Preparation Time: The Appraisal Forms should be given out to the staff member, together with a date/time for the appraisal discussion, no less than 2 weeks before the meeting in preparation for tabling at the forthcoming appraisal discussion. The staff member (or Director) may request another appraisal meeting within 10 days of the original appraisal discussion allowing time to reflect/digest views etc. The staff member can take away the Director's copy of the appraisal form for comparison and later discussion.

Director Responsible: 'John Smith' will be the Director responsible for the overall management and implementation of the scheme.

THE APPRAISAL FORM (All instructions for completion are in italics)
The appraisal form contains:

Section 1: Name, Job Title, Signatures etc.

Section 2:

i) **Job Description Objectives:** *These will, for all staff, be based on those contained in their Job Descriptions. These will be pre-typed onto each Appraisal Form before distribution.*

ii) **Job Description Key Functions:** *These will, for all staff, be based on those contained in their Job Descriptions. These will be pre-typed onto each Appraisal Form before distribution.*

iii) **Job Description Significant Relationships:** *These will, for all staff, be based on those contained in their Job Descriptions. These will be pre-typed onto each Appraisal Form before distribution.*

iv) **Team Building Dispositions:** *These are the standard Team Building Dispositions to which all teams in Ruddle Wilkinson Ltd will be working and are applicable to everyone and will be pre-typed onto the forms.*

v) **Team Key Functions:** *To remain blank until team development activities are completed*

Skills

This section lists all the skills and behaviour required to achieve the objectives/targets and fulfil the functions. There are performance indicators of 1 - 7 for each attribute to indicate the current level of performance and a matched scale 1 - 7 to indicate the future performance goals.

PERFORMANCE INDICATORS

Now	Future
1 2 3 4 5 6 7	1 2 3 4 5 6 7

1 = Seriously below average
2 = Below average
3 = Acceptable
4 = Up to standard
5 = Consistently good
6 = Constantly outstanding
7 = Exemplary

PERFORMANCE INDICATORS

Now	Future
1 2 3 4 5 6 7	1 2 3 4 5 6 7

Key Functions

1.

2.

3.

4.

5.

6.

Explanatory Notes:

Job Description Signigficant Relationships:

1.

2.

3.

4.

5.

6.

INSTRUCTIONS FOR COMPLETION OF APPRAISAL FORM:

Section 3:

Skills: *This section lists all the skills and behaviour required to achieve the job description objectives and fulfil the job description functions. Please try to be as specific as possible and avoid generalities like 'communication' by being precise, i.e. - face to face communication, written communication. In order to maintain the objectivity of this very important section it is recommended that both Director and staff member bring to the appraisal discussion any samples of work which they think exemplifies either an outstandingly good or bad demonstration of performance.*

There are performance indicators of 1 - 7 for each attribute to indicate the current level of performance and a matched scale 1 - 7 to indicate future performance goals. When this section is being completed care should be taken to ensure that the performance indicator for each skill etc. reflects not just performance at the time of writing but overall performance since the last appraisal.

SKILLS

PERFORMANCE INDICATORS
Now   Future
1 2 3 4 5 6 7   1 2 3 4 5 6 7

1=   Seriously below average
2=   Below average
3=   Acceptable
4=   Up to standard
5=   Consistently good
6=   Constantly outstanding
7=   Exemplary

PERFORMANCE INDICATORS
Now   Future
1 2 3 4 5 6 7   1 2 3 4 5 6 7

Key Functions

1.
2.
3.
4.
5.
6.

Explanatory Notes:

The Explanatory Notes are to help appraiser and appraisee to expand and illuminate the performance indicators. In this section it might be useful to cite particular examples of standard of skills.

Job Description Significant Relationships:

a.
2.
3.
4.
5.
6.

No performance indicators are required for this section but general comments about quality and usefulness of the identified significant relationships which will lead possibly to action points on page 5.

Team Building Dispositions:

PERFORMANCE INDICATORS
Now   Future
1 2 3 4 5 6 7   1 2 3 4 5 6 7

1. A resolve always to value one's
    own skills and those of others.

2. A willingness to listen and to
    communicate honestly and
    purposefully with one another.

3. A commitment to help and
    encourage one another.

4. A readiness to extend trust to one
    another's team leader, who earns this
    trust by striving to maximise the team
    welfare and performance.

5. A feeling of responsibility for the team as
    a whole as it works for the successful
    completion of a worthwhile task.

6. A willingness to contribute one's own
    creative inputs and to allow them to be
    transformed into other, better team
    outputs.

Explanatory Notes:

Behaviour   This heading focuses on appropriate and essential workplace behaviour; by and
large it is not concerned with social behaviour, but behaviour as part of performance.

PERFORMANCE INDICATORS
Now   Future
1 2 3 4 5 6 7   1 2 3 4 5 6 7

Tidyness - work station
            personal

Punctuality

Politeness/courtesy

Helpfulness

Co-operativeness

Explanatory Notes:

INSTRUCTIONS FOR COMPLETION OF APPRAISAL FORM:

PERFORMANCE INDICATORS
Now   Future
1 2 3 4 5 6 7   1 2 3 4 5 6 7

Team Building Dispositions

1. A resolve always to value one's own skills and those of others.

2. A willingness to listen and to communicate honestly and purposefully with one another.

3. A commitment to help and encourage one another.

4. A readiness to extend trust to one another's team leader, who earns this trust by striving to maximise the team welfare and performance.

5. A feeling of responsibility for the team as a whole as it works for the successful completion of a worthwhile task.

6. A willingness to contribute one's own creative inputs and to allow them to be transformed into other, better team outputs.

Explanatory Notes:

In these Explanatory Notes the appraiser and appraisee can comment on any particular features of the Team Building Dispositions and the appraisee's ability/willingness/ commitment to putting them into action.

Behaviour

This section focuses on appropriate and essential workplace behaviour; by and large it is not concerned with social behaviour, but behaviour as part of performance.

PERFORMANCE INDICATORS
Now   Future
1 2 3 4 5 6 7   1 2 3 4 5 6 7

Tidyness -   work station
               personal
Punctuality
Politeness/courtesy
Helpfulness
Co-operativeness

Explanatory Notes:

Here both the appraiser and appraisee may wish to add by prior agreement to this standard list of workplace behaviour.

Overall Comments and Summary

INSTRUCTIONS FOR COMPLETION OF APPRAISAL FORM:

Section 4:

Overall Comments and Summary

On this page the appraiser and appraisee should comment on any points which have not been captured hitherto or use this as an opportunity to expand descriptively on areas for development and enhancement.

Development Action

In this section staff member and Director are asked to indicate what development actions are required to achieve the skills/behaviour goals in Section 3.

ORDER OF PRIORITY IF REQUIRED	TOPIC	FUTURE PERFORMANCE GOAL	DEVELOPMENT METHOD	WITH WHOM	BY DATE

The above are all to be reviewed during an agreed period of regular, documented supervision.

INSTRUCTIONS FOR COMPLETION OF APPRAISAL FORM:

Section 5:

Development Action

In this section the staff member and Director are asked to indicate what development actions are required to achieve the performance goals in Section 3.

ORDER OF PRIORITY IF REQUIRED	TOPIC	FUTURE PERFORMANCE GOAL	DEVELOPMENT METHOD	WITH WHOM	BY DATE
For example: *By end of month*	*Work station tidyness*	*4*	*Personal commitment*	*Line Manager*	*31/7/96*

Appraiser and appraisee may choose to rank in order of priority the sequence in which the topics for development action may be tackled. This is at their discretion and for discussion and agreement.

The Development actions should be monitored at regular, documented, individual supervisory sessions, held at appropriate agreed intervals, i.e. weekly, fortnightly, monthly etc.

This section should be completed by the Director and the staff member, with the Director making suggestions about useful actions to achieve future personal goals. These actions should be: S M A R T

S - ENSIBLE
-
M - EASURABLE
-
A - CHIEVABLE
-
R - ELEVANT
-
T - IMED

This back page is to be copied, one for the appraiser and one for the appraisee, before the whole Appraisal Form is handed to 'John Smith' for confidential filing.

Bibliography

Anderson, A. and Tobbell, G. (1983) *Costing Training Centre*, IMS Report No. 72.

Baron, B. (1981) *Managing Human Resources* (eds Cowling, A.G. and Mailer, C.), Arnold.

Bennett, R. and Leduchowicz, T. (1983) *What Makes an Effective Trainer?*, MCB University Press.

Fletcher, C. and Williams, R. (1985) *Performance Appraisal and Career Development*, Hutchinson.

Honey, P. (1990) *How to Manage your Learning Environment*;

Honey, P. (1988) *101 Ways to Develop your People, Without Really Trying*;

Honey, P. (1986) *The Manual of Learning Opportunities*
(all of the above are available by mail order from Peter Honey Publications, tel: 01628 33946, fax: 01628 33262)

Hudson, H. (1992) *The Perfect Appraisal*, Arrow Business Books.

IPM (now Institute of Personnel and Development) (1983) *A Positive Policy for Training and Development*, IPM.

McGregor, D. (1960) *The Human Side of the Enterprise*, McGraw-Hill.

Pepper, A.D. (1984) *Managing the Training and Development Function*, Gower Press.

Turrell, M. (1980) *Training Analysis: A Guide to Recognising Training Needs*, Macdonald & Evans.